Theory Paper Grade 6 2015 A
Model Answers

1   *There are many ways of completing this question. Either of the specimen completions below would receive full marks.* (15)

EITHER

(a)   *Chords are shown here with roman numerals AND notes on the stave. EITHER of these methods of notation would receive full marks. Other recognized methods of notation will also be considered and marks awarded accordingly.*

OR

(b)

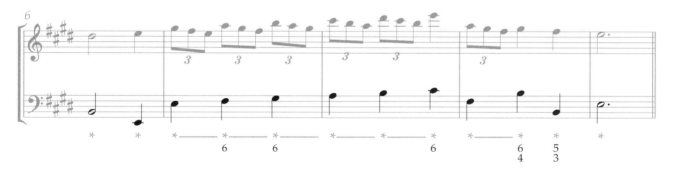

2   *There are many ways of completing this question. The specimen completion below would receive full marks.* (15)

3 *There are many ways of completing this question. Either of the specimen completions below would receive full marks.* (20)
*The given openings are printed in grey in order to distinguish them from the completion, but candidates must
include the opening in their answer.*

EITHER

(a) flute
   Source: Schubert, String Trio in B♭ D. 471

OR

(b) trombone

4

4   *Source: Boismortier, Sonata in E minor Op. 19 No. 2*

(a)   *All possible answers are shown on the extract reproduced below. For full marks, candidates need to identify only one example of each answer.*

B	Bars	8–9	(2)
C	Bar	10 / 12	(2)
D	Bars	7–8	(2)

(b)   X   appoggiatura / leaning note   (2)
　　　Y   unaccented passing note   (2)
　　　Z   note of anticipation   (2)

(c)

(3)

(d)   Bar 2   ii°⁷b / II⁷b diminished / iv⁶a / IV⁶a minor   Key   E minor   (4)
　　　Bar 4   V⁷a / V⁷a major   Key   B minor   (4)

(e)   　　1650–1750   (1)

use of keyboard (not piano) / bass line typical of Baroque period / Baroque harmonic   (1)
　　language / lack of dynamics

5   (a)   divided / divided into two parts   (2)
              suddenly   (2)

        (b)   (i)      (3)

               (ii)      (4)

        (c)   (i)   cellos; fourth horn; second bassoon   (3)
               (ii)   violas; first clarinet; cor anglais   (3)
               (iii)   flute   (2)

        (d)   1   perfect 5th   (2)
               2   augmented 4th   (2)

        (e)   *One mark will be awarded (up to a maximum of two marks) for each correct reference to the following:*
               no strings / no brass / soft dynamic in orchestra / low tessitura   (2)

Theory Paper Grade 6   2015   B
Model Answers

1   *There are many ways of completing this question. Either of the specimen completions below would receive full marks.* (15)

EITHER

(a)   *Chords are shown here with roman numerals AND notes on the stave. EITHER of these methods of notation would receive full marks. Other recognized methods of notation will also be considered and marks awarded accordingly.*

OR

(b)

2   *There are many ways of completing this question. The specimen completion below would receive full marks.*   (15)

3   *There are many ways of completing this question. Either of the specimen completions below would receive full marks.*   (20)
The given openings are printed in grey in order to distinguish them from the completion, but candidates must
include the opening in their answer.

EITHER

(a)   violin
   Source: Schubert, String Trio in B♭ D. 581

OR

(b)   flute

4 *Source: G. Pinto, Piano Sonata in E♭ minor Op. 3 No. 1, second movement*

(a)   *All possible answers are shown on the extract reproduced below.*

B	Bar	10	(2)
C	Bar	9	(2)
D	Bars	20–22	(2)
E	Bar	21 / 23	(2)

(b)   Similarity   melodic shape   (1)

One mark will be awarded (up to a maximum of three marks) for each correct reference to the following:
Differences   harmony / cresc. in bar 11 / rhythm / phrasing   (3)

(c)

(3)

(d) Bar 2   V⁷a / V⁷a major   Key   A♭ major   (4)
    Bar 15 ii°⁷b / II⁷b diminished / iv⁶a / IV⁶a minor   Key   F minor   (4)

(e) true   (2)

5 (a) with vigour / animated   (2)
      both players   (2)
      play each printed quaver as two semiquavers   (2)
      roll / drum roll / rapid reiteration of the same note   (2)

  (b) *All possible answers are shown on the extract reproduced below.*

      B   Bar 6   (2)
      C   Bar 7   (2)
      D   Bar 5   (2)

Sibelius

(c)　(i)

(3)

(ii)

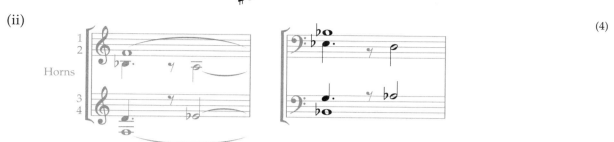

(4)

(d)　1　diminished 5th

(2)

　2　minor 2nd

(2)

Theory Paper Grade 6　2015　C
Model Answers

1　*There are many ways of completing this question. Either of the specimen completions below would receive full marks.* (15)

EITHER

(a)　*Chords are shown here with roman numerals AND notes on the stave. EITHER of these methods of notation would receive full marks. Other recognized methods of notation will also be considered and marks awarded accordingly.*

OR

(b)

2   *There are many ways of completing this question. The specimen completion below would receive full marks.*   (15)

3   *There are many ways of completing this question. Either of the specimen completions below would receive full marks.* (20)
The given openings are printed in grey in order to distinguish them from the completion, but candidates must include the opening in their answer.

EITHER

(a)   oboe
      Source: Haydn, String Quartet in E minor Op. 17 No. 1, third movement

OR

(b)   cello

4   (a)   spirited / with spirit   (2)
             getting much slower / gradually getting much slower   (2)

      (b)   Bar 8   ii°⁷a / II⁷a diminished / iv⁶d / IV⁶d minor   Key   D minor   (4)
             Bar 17   V⁷a / V⁷a major   Key   G minor   (4)

(c) *One mark will be awarded (up to a maximum of three marks) for each correct reference to the following:*
change of key / faster tempo / quaver movement / less sustained / articulation   (3)

(d) *All possible answers are shown on the extract reproduced below*

     B   Bar 17   (2)
     C   Bar 22   (2)
     D   Bar 23   (2)

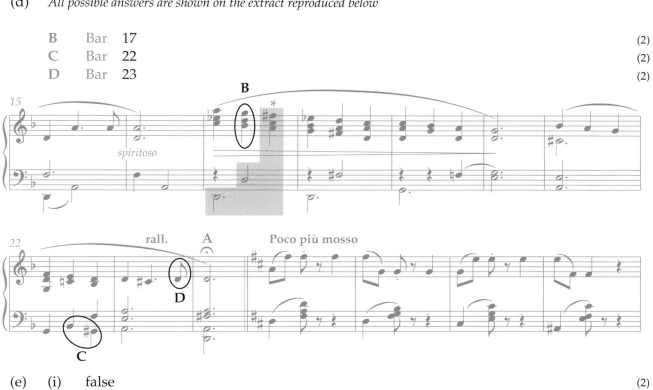

(e) (i)   false   (2)
     (ii) false   (2)

5 (a)   with movement / with motion / moving   (2)
        with the bow / bowed   (2)

    (b)   B   Bars 4–5 / 5–6   (2)

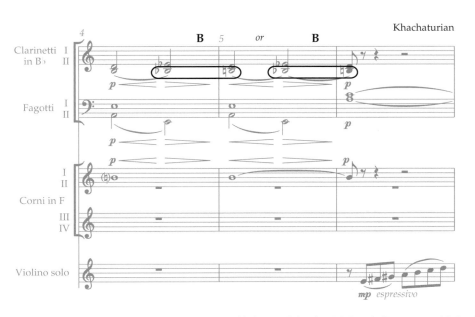

C Bar **11** (2)

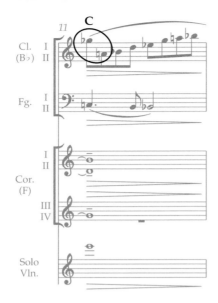

D Bar **7** (2)

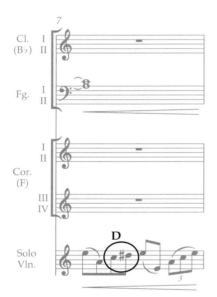

(c) (i) (4)

(ii) (3)

(d) (i) violas (2)
    (ii) E; solo violin (2)
    (iii) major 6th (2)

(e) true (2)

Theory Paper Grade 6   2015   S
Model Answers

1   *There are many ways of completing this question. Either of the specimen completions below would receive full marks.* (15)

EITHER

(a)   *Chords are shown here with roman numerals AND notes on the stave. EITHER of these methods of notation would receive full marks. Other recognized methods of notation will also be considered and marks awarded accordingly.*

OR

(b)

2   *There are many ways of completing this question. The specimen completion below would receive full marks.*   (15)

3   *There are many ways of completing this question. Either of the specimen completions below would receive full marks.* (20)
*The given openings are printed in grey in order to distinguish them from the completion, but candidates must
include the opening in their answer.*

EITHER

(a)   clarinet
    Source: Haydn, String Quartet in G Op. 64 No. 4

OR

(b)   cello

4   *Source: Beethoven, Piano Sonata in F Op. 10 No. 2*

(a)   Bar 7   V⁷d / V⁷d major   Key   B♭ major   (4)
    Bar 10   iib / IIb minor   Key   F major   (4)

(b)   (3)

(c) *All possible answers are shown on the extract reproduced below. For full marks, candidates need to identify only one example of each answer.*

        B   Bar   26   (2)
        C   Bar(s) 28 / 28–29   (2)
        D   Bar(s) 21 / 25 / 29   (2)

(d)   reinforced / reinforcing   (2)

(e)   Similarity   rhythm   (1)

    One mark will be awarded (up to a maximum of three marks) for each correct reference to the following:
    Differences   an octave higher in bars 27–28 / dynamics / slur in bars 19–20 /   (3)
                               texture of chords / C♯ in bar 28

(f)   Beethoven   (1)

    Classical harmonic language / use of piano discounts Handel / use of dynamics   (1)

5   (a)   plucked   (2)
             divided / divided into two parts   (2)

    (b)   (i)   second violins; second clarinet   (2)
             (ii)   oboe / cor anglais / double bassoon   (2)
             (iii)   fourth horn   (2)

(c)   (i)   (4)

       (ii)   (3)

(d)   1   major 10th / compound major 3rd   (2)
       2   perfect 12th / compound perfect 5th   (2)

(e)   (i)   true   (2)
       (ii)   true   (2)

Music Theory Past Papers 2015 Model Answers

Model answers for four past papers from ABRSM's 2015 Theory exams for Grade 6

Key features:

- a list of correct answers where appropriate
- a selection of likely options where the answer can be expressed in a variety of ways
- a single exemplar where a composition-style answer is required

Support material for ABRSM Theory exams

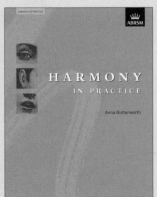
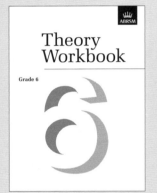

ABRSM is the exam board of the Royal Schools of Music. We are committed to actively supporting high-quality music-making, learning and development throughout the world, and to producing the best possible resources for music teachers and students.

ABRSM
24 Portland Place
London W1B 1LU
United Kingdom

www.abrsm.org

ISBN 978-1-84849-752-8

9 781848 497528